HEADLINE SERIES

No. 324   FOREIGN POLICY ASSOCIATION   Fall 2002

NATO and Transatlantic Relations in the 21st Century: Crisis, Continuity or Change?

Cover Design: Agnes Kostro $5.95
Cover Photo: AP/Wide World Photos

The Author

STANLEY R. SLOAN is a private consultant, visiting scholar at Middlebury College, and director of the Atlantic Community Initiative (see Online Resources in Talking It Over section). In 1999 he retired from his position as senior specialist in International Security Policy with the Congressional Research Service. He had previously served as an officer in the U.S. Air Force and as an analyst at the Central Intelligence Agency.  He received an MIA from Columbia University's School of International Affairs and is the author of many books and articles on foreign and defense policy. His latest book is *NATO, the European Union and the Atlantic Community: The Transatlantic Bargain Reconsidered*.

The Foreign Policy Association

The Foreign Policy Association is a private, nonprofit, nonpartisan educational organization. Its purpose is to stimulate wider interest and more effective participation in, and greater understanding of, world affairs among American citizens. Among its activities is the continuous publication, dating from 1935, of the HEADLINE SERIES. The author is responsible for factual accuracy and for the views expressed. FPA itself takes no position on issues of U.S. foreign policy.

HEADLINE SERIES (ISSN 0017-8780) is published occasionally by the Foreign Policy Association, Inc., 470 Park Avenue So., New York, NY 10016. Chairman, Dave Williams; President, Noel V. Lateef; Editor in Chief, Karen M. Rohan; Managing Editor, Ann R. Monjo; Associate Editors, Nicholas Y. Barratt and Agnes Kostro. Subscription rates, $20.00 for 4 issues. Single copy price $5.95; double issue $11.25; special issue $10.95. Discount 25% on 10 to 99 copies; 30% on 100 to 499; 35% on 500 and over. Payment must accompany all orders. Postage and handling: $3.00 for first copy; $.50 each additional copy. For foreign subscriptions please add $9.00 for shipping and handling. Second-class postage paid at New York, NY, and additional mailing offices. POSTMASTER: Send address changes to HEADLINE SERIES, Foreign Policy Association, 470 Park Avenue So., New York, NY 10016. Copyright 2002 by Foreign Policy Association, Inc. Design by Agnes Kostro. Printed at Science Press, Ephrata, Pennsylvania. Published Fall 2002.

Library of Congress Control Number: 2002114139
ISBN 0-87124-205-2

Introduction

THE TRANSATLANTIC ALLIANCE between the United States,
Canada and Europe has been a vital foundation for U.S.
foreign policy and a key stabilizing factor in international relations for over 50 years. The North Atlantic Treaty, signed in
Washington, D.C. in 1949, created the North Atlantic Treaty
Organization (NATO), which throughout the cold war (1947–
89) helped counter the power of the Soviet Union in Europe
and prevent the spread of communism. Since the end of the
cold war and the dissolution of the Soviet Union, NATO has
been adapted with the goal of preparing it to take on the new
challenges to peace and security. The alliance has played a
major role in the Balkans, helping enforce peace there, and now
is working to become more relevant to the challenges posed by

terrorism and weapons of mass destruction. NATO has opened its doors to new democracies in Central and Eastern Europe and, at the same time, has intensified its relationship with Russia.

In spite of this record of accomplishment and adaptation, a crisis of confidence in the alliance appears to have emerged at the beginning of the twenty-first century. That crisis has grown out of strategic changes in international relations, a gap between U.S. and European military capabilities, divergent perspectives on issues as varied as terrorism, the Middle East policy conundrum, policy toward Iraq, and economic competition among the allies.

NATO has survived many such "crises" in its history, including those brought on by the defeat of the European Defense Community in 1954, France's announced departure from NATO's integrated military command structure in 1966, differences between the United States and Europe about the Soviet invasion of Afghanistan in 1979 and over deployment of intermediate-range nuclear forces in Europe in the early 1980s. On each occasion, the allies have found their way out of disagreement and moved on to revalidate their alliance.

The question now is whether or not the United States and its European allies have the political will not only to resolve their current differences but to emerge from the process with a stronger, more relevant transatlantic relationship.

This HEADLINE SERIES examines the background of the current crisis in the alliance, discusses issues now facing the transatlantic allies, and considers the options and likely futures for transatlantic relations.

1

Issues Facing the Alliance

THE CURRENT CRISIS in transatlantic relations is in many ways an old issue in a new setting. The original goal of a "balanced" alliance in terms of burdens and responsibilities was never achieved during the cold war. In the post-cold-war period, new attempts by Europe to increase its role in the alliance have been given impetus by the deepening process of European integration. However, these efforts have been frustrated by the emergence of the United States as the world superpower, possessing global military capabilities at a time when Europe's military spending remains depressed and its focus is on developing "civilian" power.

Role of the U.S. War on Terrorism

The current malaise in the alliance was brought to a head by the September 11, 2001, terrorist attacks on the United States, organized by the Al Qaeda radical Islamic group, and by the U.S. response to those attacks.

President George W. Bush declared war on terrorism, and the United States prepared to mount a campaign against the Taliban leadership and forces in Afghanistan that had hosted and supported the Al Qaeda organization and its leader, Osama bin Laden.

Within 24 hours of the attacks on the United States, the North Atlantic Council (NAC, comprising representatives of all NATO countries) decided to invoke Article 5 of the NATO treaty, which commits members to regard an attack on one as an attack on all, if it was determined that a foreign source was responsible for the attacks, not domestic terrorism. On October 2, 2001, NATO Secretary General Lord Robertson announced the allies had concluded the attacks had been directed from abroad and therefore would be regarded as covered by Article 5.

The United States made it clear that the alliance's declaration of an Article 5 response was appreciated, but Washington would conduct military operations itself, with ad hoc coalitions of willing countries. The Bush Administration had decided not to ask that military operations be conducted through the NATO integrated command structure. Such a request would have created serious political dilemmas for many allies. The discussion of NATO's area of operation had basically been put aside since the debates leading up to NATO's 1999 strategic concept (a statement of NATO's goals and how best to pursue them), and there was no enthusiasm for reopening the issue in the middle of this crisis. Furthermore, the United States obviously preferred to keep tight control of any military operations.

Nonetheless, NATO was asked to provide a number of services on behalf of the war against terrorism. On October 4, NATO allies agreed to enhance bilateral and NATO intelli-

An AWACS military plane takes off from a NATO airbase in Germany. Five AWACS planes with European pilots and crews were deployed from Germany to Oklahoma on October 12, 2001, to help protect U.S. skies.

gence-sharing, assist allies facing terrorist threats because of the counterterror campaign, grant blanket overflight clearances for the U.S. and other allied aircraft involved in counterterror operations, and make airfields and ports available to support operations against terror.

The NAC agreed that the alliance was prepared to deploy elements of its Standing Naval Forces to the eastern Mediterranean in order to provide a NATO presence and demonstrate resolve. On October 8, NATO announced that allied AWACS (Airborne Warning and Control System) aircraft would be deployed to the United States to help patrol airspace. The move freed up U.S. forces for use in the air war against Taliban forces in Afghanistan. This was the first time NATO assets had been used in direct support of the continental United States. (The operation was discontinued in mid-May 2002).

The terrorist attack and the actions required to respond militarily demonstrated in many ways the wisdom of the adaptation of the alliance that had been under way since the early 1990s. NATO never abandoned the critical Article 5 commitment, but began preparing for the new kind of security challenges alliance members thought likely in the twenty-first century. NATO needed more forces capable of being moved quickly to conflicts beyond national borders and prepared to fight in a variety of topographic and climatic conditions, using a mix of conventional and high-tech weaponry.

Preparing for and conducting operations in Afghanistan, the U.S. Administration sought help from the allies mainly through bilateral channels. In the weeks following the attacks, some Pentagon officials privately dismissed NATO's formal invocation of the alliance's mutual defense provision and complained that the alliance was not relevant to the new challenges posed by the counterterror campaign.

NATO's initial response therefore left many questions unanswered about the future of the allied response to the terrorist challenge and to the other issues that remained on the alliance platter. Would NATO countries follow up their Article 5 commitment with resources that would be helpful in the conduct of a far-reaching and long-running campaign against international terrorism? Would the NATO cooperative framework prove helpful or would it be seen by the United States as inappropriate and unhelpful for the kinds of operations required by the war on terror? How would the new circumstances created by the terrorist attacks and their aftermath affect other key issues for the alliance, including NATO's future role in the Balkans, coordination of U.S., allied and NATO approaches to ballistic-missile defense, relations with Russia, continuation of the alliance-enlargement process, and future development of the Common European Security and Defense Policy (CESDP)?

In the aftermath of the terrorist attacks, Charles Grant, a British defense expert, judged that the U.S. choice not to use NATO to run the military operations against terrorist targets in Afghanistan means "it's unlikely the Americans will ever again wish to use NATO to manage a major shooting war." Allied officials complained that, after showing their support and willingness to contribute, the United States largely proceeded with a strategy focusing on dividing, not sharing, responsibilities. According to press reports, the situation irritated European leaders who, having given their strong political support, felt embarrassed about invoking Article 5 and then being left on the sidelines. One French official reportedly observed that the message from the United States was "We'll do the cooking and prepare what people are going to eat, then you will wash the dirty dishes."

U.S. and European Roles

To some extent, the situation can be attributed to factors for which the Europeans themselves are to blame. First, they did not, for the most part, have significant military assets to contribute to the first phase of the Afghan campaign, which relied heavily on air-delivered, precision-guided munitions. Second, officials in the Bush Administration were fully aware of past NATO-nation resistance to involving the alliance in military operations beyond their borders, to say nothing of beyond Europe.

On the other hand, it appeared that the United States missed an opportunity to move the NATO consensus well beyond the 1999 strategic concept following the September 11 events. A political consensus existed that could have been used to expand NATO's horizons and establish a mechanism for NATO contributions in the future. If the war against international terrorism remains for some years the main focus of U.S. security policy, NATO's ability to be part of the solution could exert a major influence on U.S. perceptions of the alliance's utility and European perceptions of the U.S. commitment to transatlantic defense cooperation.

Power relationships between the United States and Europe

have changed fundamentally over the years. Since the end of the cold war, the "West" has seemed relatively stable while the former "East" has experienced revolutionary changes. This appearance of stability, however, has partially concealed fundamental structural changes in the roles of the two key Western power centers, the United States and the European Union, (EU, currently consisting of 15 member states ranging from Greece to Sweden and Ireland to Italy). The United States has become the only true global superpower, with military capacities backed up by economic resources and political influence unmatched by any other country. The EU is a long way from being a coherent international actor, to say nothing of a full political, economic and military union, but it has nonetheless become a unique and important player on the international scene.

These evolutionary changes have created both new prospects and increased tensions. Even though the United States complained loudly about Europe's inability to shoulder its "fair share" of defense burdens during the cold war, Washington at the same time became accustomed to its dominant leadership position. Now, in spite of the huge gap in military capabilities between the United States and Europe, the EU is in a position to use its diplomatic skills, backed by economic clout, to play a unique role in international affairs. For example, when it appeared that the United States was unwilling or unable to play an active mediating role in the Middle East in 2001-2002, the EU sent its foreign policy representative, Javier Solana, to try to promote peace. The effort was unsuccessful, but did help stimulate resumption of a more active U.S. role in the conflict.

The dominant international role of the United States can be a positive influence, if U.S. power is used judiciously. On the other hand, too heavy a U.S. hand, whether in military intervention, exercise of political influence, or insistence on getting its way in economic matters, almost immediately raises concerns about U.S. "hegemony" or excess influence on the affairs of other sovereign states.

The new European clout can add to the tools of the Western

by Wright for the Palm Beach Post, Fla.

community of democracies in promoting international economic development, conflict resolution and international stability. However, if the Europeans overreach their grasp, and try to accomplish more than their level of internal unity will support, or if they work openly against U.S. international policies, they will create more problems than they will solve.

The September 11 attacks on the United States and the subsequent "war on terrorism" illuminated the extent to which the growing gap between U.S. and European military power created divergent approaches to the use of force in international affairs.

Robert Kagan, a politically conservative American commentator, has argued that the imbalance between U.S. and European military power has created a wide divergence in transatlantic attitudes toward the use of force. Kagan points out that when the United States was a young, weak nation, it relied heavily on international law and agreements to protect its interests, while the more powerful Europeans guarded their flexibility to act. Today, with the power distribution reversed, so are the attitudes. The United States now carries the "big stick" internationally and is not anxious to have its potential use constrained when "justice" requires action.

Kagan argues that the success of the integration process in Western Europe has created a new "ideology" on which Europeans largely base their role in the world, featuring cooperation and diplomacy rather than power politics and coercion: "This is what many Europeans believe they have to offer the world: not power, but the transcendence of power." Kagan sees this as Europe's new civilizing mission in the world, including the United States. He judges that "America's power, and its willingness to exercise that power—unilaterally if necessary—represents a threat to Europe's new sense of mission."

It clearly would overstate the case to argue that Europeans have rejected the use of force as a tool of international relations. European governments did not hesitate to put their troops in harm's way in Afghanistan and European special forces, for example, have fought with distinction alongside U.S. and Canadian troops there.

Allies Do Have Differing Attitudes

However, it does appear that military capabilities and experience do influence attitudes toward the use of force. What to do about Iraq's president, Saddam Hussein, and his alleged programs to develop weapons of mass destruction is a case in point. The United States can at least imagine removing Saddam's dictatorial regime by force, because it has the military capability to do so—perhaps even without the help of allies. The Europeans would much prefer to exhaust all nonmilitary options, including diplomacy, sanctions and promises of assistance for a post-Saddam Iraq, before resorting to an attack on Iraq. In a nonmilitary approach, the Europeans would have influence and a degree of control over the policy. In a military approach, the United States would dominate decisionmaking even though the consequences—good or bad—would have important implications for European interests.

Oct. 10, 2001: NATO Secretary General Lord Robertson confers at White House with President George W. Bush about the antiterrorism effort and U.S. military action in Afghanistan.

There is a gap in political philosophies as well as in military capabilities underlying today's crisis in transatlantic ties and it remains to be seen if this gap can be overcome by changes in government policies. But many analysts believe that the basic transatlantic relationship remains intact and relevant. The United States, Canada and the European democracies still remain determined to "safeguard the freedom, common heritage and civilization of their peoples, founded on the principles of democracy, individual liberty and the rule of law," as proclaimed in the preamble to the North Atlantic Treaty. However, the transatlantic allies have always implemented these broad principles differently. European governments support a much stronger safety net for those who fall through the cracks of the social and economic system than does the United States.

On the other hand, the United States appears to present many more opportunities for advancement and economic gain based on individual initiative rather than family or social status. "Democracy" is practiced in different ways. All European democracies have governments led by prime ministers based on majorities in the national parliaments. In the United States, the head of government—the President, who is also head of state—can be from one party while one or both houses of Congress are controlled by the other, according to the U.S. Constitution.

In recent years, transatlantic divisions have emerged over a number of social and moral issues. European governments overwhelmingly reject the death penalty as cruel and inhuman, while the majority of Americans still apparently feel it is a necessary tool for the justice system. Significant elements of U.S. agribusiness have accepted using seeds that are genetically modified to protect crops against insects and disease. Europeans, as well as growing numbers of Americans, reject such modification as potentially unsafe and creating "unfair" advantages in agricultural trade. Such divisions, however, can be exaggerated as "transatlantic differences" since they are also divisive inside the United States and Europe, as well as across the Atlantic.

Economic Cooperation and Conflict

The United States and Europe share immense trade and financial interests. The members of the EU have over $800 billion of direct investment in the United States. The United States has over $573 billion invested in EU states. The EU and the United States together account for more than 30 percent of world trade and represent almost 60 percent of the industrialized world's gross domestic product.

The United States and the EU members, along with Japan, are the key players in the Western economic system. They compete with one another for markets and resources; they use their laws and regulations to protect domestic producers or to give them advantages in the international marketplace, sometimes under the cover of protecting health or saving the environment.

Over the years, the United States, Europe and other market economies have negotiated arrangements to limit the degree to which governments assist their domestic industries. They have limited the role of tariffs in international trade, benefiting consumers around the world, and negotiated a complex set of rules and procedures to ensure "fair" trade practices. The World Trade Organization, which came into being in 1995 as a successor to the General Agreement on Tariffs and Trade, now provides the framework for adjudicating disputes and settling differences over trade issues. However, governments have retained a number of tools designed to assist domestic industries in preserving jobs and protecting endangered industrial sectors and, not incidentally, to win domestic political support.

At the end of the cold war, a number of pundits observed that the Soviet threat had imposed a discipline on U.S. and European trade and financial relations that would disappear in the post-cold-war era. According to this view, trade differences that had been controlled because of the confrontation with Moscow would break out in the open with a devastating impact on transatlantic relations. It was also speculated that the creation of a European currency (the euro), which would eventually compete with the U.S. dollar for domination of international financial markets, would create political tensions across the Atlantic.

Even though the United States and Europe have continued to struggle with a variety of trade issues—most recently including U.S.-imposed tariffs on steel imports and increased subsidies for U.S. farmers—such differences have not shaken the foundations of the relationship. This is so because the United States and Europe remain committed to resolution of their differences in ways that balance costs and benefits over time.

In 2002, EU members were particularly disappointed that a Republican Administration in Washington, expected to be a big advocate of free trade, tended to be highly protectionist.

Europeans understand the domestic political motivations for the Bush Administration's actions, but their experience with previous Republican Administrations had led them to have higher expectations.

Perhaps the most important problem is that the European allies see U.S. trade policy as suggesting the United States will go its own way, irrespective of the views of its allies or the consequences for their interests. Europeans for many years have been critical of what they see as U.S. excessive consumption of energy and lack of concern for the impact of modern economies on the environment. The Bush Administration's rejection of the Kyoto Protocol to combat global warming has reinforced this perception.

The bottom line is that U.S.-European economic issues have contributed to the broader sense of crisis in the relationship, even if they have not been the primary cause. As economist C. Fred Bergsten has written, "The United States simply cannot dominate the world economy as it does global security affairs, and Europe is its only potential partner, in terms of both capability and cultural compatibility.... Both need...to start thinking in terms of cooperating and indeed coordinating consistently, both to minimize the problems they cause each other and to provide progressive leadership for the world."

2

Origins and Evolution
of the Alliance

The "TRANSATLANTIC BARGAIN"—a term originally used by Harlan Cleveland, a former U.S. representative to NATO, to describe the compact between the United States and Europe—was a pact between the United States and its original European partners, with the militarily modest but politically important participation of Canada. The U.S. Congress actively took part in shaping and overseeing the agreement, given the crucial constitutional roles of the Senate in the process of ratifying treaties and the House of Representa-

NATO MEMBERSHIP

■ **NATO members** (U.S. and Canada not shown)

1949—Belgium, Britain, Canada, Denmark, France, Iceland, Italy, Luxembourg, the Netherlands, Norway, Portugal and the United States (12)

1951—Greece and Turkey (2)

1955—West Germany (1)

1982—Spain (1)

1999—The Czech Republic, Hungary and Poland (3)

*May 2002: NATO-Russia Council established

NATO applicants: Albania, Bulgaria, Croatia, Estonia, Latvia, Lithuania, Macedonia, Romania, Slovenia, Slovakia

tives in legislating funding for government programs. The arrangement was that the United States would contribute to the defense of Europe and to Europe's economic recovery from the war if the Europeans would organize themselves to help defend against the Soviet threat and use the economic aid efficiently.

The European allies were quite successful in carrying out the second half of the deal. In 1947, the Organization for European Economic Cooperation (OEEC) was created to coordinate utilization of Marshall Plan recovery assistance from the United States and to promote European economic cooperation. The first step toward true European integration was the European Coal and Steel Community (ECSC, formed in 1951) followed in 1957 by the Treaty of Rome, which established the European Economic Community (EEC) and the European Atomic Energy Community (Euratom), the precursors of today's European Union.

The allies were not nearly so successful in the security area. In 1950 France had proposed creation of a European Defense Community (EDC) to organize Europe's military contribution to NATO. When that initiative failed in 1954, the arrangements put in place of the EDC left the transatlantic bargain highly dependent on U.S. nuclear weapons and a substantial U.S. military presence in Europe.

Throughout the cold war, the alliance lived with the 1954 "revision" and a persistent burden-sharing debate between the United States and its European allies, as well as between successive U.S. Administrations and the U.S. Congress.

The involvement of the Congress in NATO affairs, judiciously sought by President Harry S. Truman's Administration in the late 1940s, ensured a solid foundation for U.S. participation. But it also guaranteed that senators and congressmen would for the life of the NATO treaty closely inspect its terms and conditions. Congress has found burden-sharing lacking for most of NATO's existence—right up to today.

There have been many subordinate provisos that were more

important to individual allies than to the United States. France wanted to ensure that it would not have to face, on its own, a resurgence of German power. Britain wanted U.S. participation in European defense to provide an effective deterrent to Soviet expansionism so as to leave British assets to maintain the country's position as a global power. Canada wanted the agreement to be about more than military power, of which it had little, and more about political values, which it held high. When the Federal Republic of Germany joined NATO, it accepted constraints on its military capabilities in return for sovereignty over its internal affairs.

NATO has always been more than simply a defensive alliance. The North Atlantic Treaty provides a broad and flexible mandate to defend and promote allied interests and security. Moreover, preserving the attributes of a collective defense system, including an integrated command structure, a defense-planning process and thoroughgoing political and military consultations, strengthens NATO's ability to play new roles and assume new missions that respond to the post-cold-war challenges.

A Community of Values

The North Atlantic Treaty was designed to counter Soviet expansion and military power. But the treaty itself was based on common values, identified no enemy, protected the sovereign decisionmaking rights of all members, and was written in sufficiently flexible language to facilitate adjustments to accommodate changing international circumstances. British Foreign Secretary Ernest Bevin, one of NATO's "founding fathers," urged the creation of a "Western Union" in a speech to the British Parliament on January 22, 1948. He asserted that "our sacrifices during the war, our hatred of injustice and oppression, our party democracy, our striving for economic rights and our conception and love of liberty are common among us all." During negotiation of the treaty, Canada argued the need to reflect "the ideological unity of the North Atlantic powers."

U.S. Secretary of State Dean Acheson subsequently maintained that "the central idea of the treaty is not a static one..." and that "the North Atlantic Treaty is far more than a defensive arrangement. It is an affirmation of the moral and spiritual values which we hold in common." During 1949 Senate hearings on the treaty, Acheson and other Truman Administration witnesses argued that what they were proposing was very different from previous military-alliance systems.

What made NATO different was that the treaty's preamble clearly articulated support for "democracy, individual liberty and the rule of law." During the cold war, these values occasionally took second place when the United States and its allies tolerated authoritarian regimes in NATO in the interest of maintaining a militarily strong alliance. But NATO's survival beyond the end of the cold war suggested that its value foundation and the inherent logic of Euro-Atlantic cooperation remained important ingredients in the glue that holds the alliance together. These same factors have made NATO membership attractive to the new European democracies. The question is whether or not the value foundation remains as strong today as it was in 1949 or during the cold war.

Broad and Flexible Mandate

The treaty's relatively simple language does not spell out in great detail how its objectives should be implemented. There is no specified military strategy, no requirement for any particular organization or even military arrangements, beyond the creation of a North Atlantic Council and a defense committee. This suggests substantial latitude for adaptation and adjustment to changing circumstances. The only limits on such changes are imposed by national interests, values, inertia and other human and institutional factors, not by the treaty.

NATO's flexibility was demonstrated, for example, by the military buildup and elaboration of an integrated command structure in the early 1950s, which had not been anticipated when the treaty was signed, and was judged necessary only after North Korea invaded South Korea. The alliance was adjusted again following the failure of the European Defense Community (EDC). In the mid-1960s, NATO was forced to adapt to France's departure from the integrated command structure. In 1967, the allies revamped NATO's military strategy and approved the Harmel Report, produced by a committee under the chairmanship of the Belgian foreign minister, Pierre Harmel, which gave the alliance the mission of promoting détente as well as sustaining deterrence and defense. And, in the 1990s, the allies reoriented NATO's goals and activities to take into account the peaceful revolutions that brought democracy to Eastern and Central Europe and gave Russia, Ukraine and other former Soviet republics the opportunity for independence and democratic reform. Some now argue, however, that NATO's political flexibility is leading toward its military irrelevance.

A Collective Defense System

At NATO's founding, the most prominent aspect of the treaty was its requirement for individual and collective actions for defense against armed attack. Article 3 of the treaty provides that the allies "separately and jointly, by means of continuous and effective self-help and mutual aid, will maintain and develop their individual and collective capacity to resist armed attack." In Article 5, the treaty's collective defense provision, the parties agreed that "an armed attack against one or more of them in Europe or North America shall be considered an attack against them all" and that each party to the treaty would "assist the party or parties so attacked by taking forthwith, individually and in concert with the other parties, such action as it deems necessary, including the use of armed force, to restore and maintain the security of the North Atlantic area."

During the cold war, NATO's strategy and the way in which the United States, Canada and Britain deployed their forces on the Continent gave Article 5 more substance in practice than suggested by the words in the treaty. Beginning in the early

1950s, the United States deployed its military forces and nuclear weapons forward in Europe, mainly in Germany, in a way that ensured a Soviet attack on the West would in its early stages engage U.S. forces, therefore constituting an attack on the United States as well as on the nation directly attacked.

Most activities of the alliance have a goal of defense cooperation that lies beyond collective defense, even though the institutions and processes developed to implement collective defense, including the integrated command structure, remain critically important to NATO's future.

NATO and Crisis Management

At the end of the cold war, the allies asked themselves if they still needed an elaborate system of political and military cooperation at a time when the Soviet threat had all but vanished. Their answer, in the November 1991 New Strategic Concept, was that political consultation and defense cooperation, so essential in the cold war, could be broadened to include other purposes. NATO cooperation was widely accepted as having facilitated an effective U.S.-led coalition response to Iraq's invasion of Kuwait and the experience had a significant influence on the directions taken in the 1991 strategic concept. Since that time, most of NATO's military activities have been focused on "non-Article 5" requirements, most significantly in the Balkans. The mandate for such activities is found primarily in Article 4 of the North Atlantic Treaty, which authorizes cooperation to deal with circumstances that "threaten" the security of one or more NATO members.

NATO remains an organization of sovereign nation-states in which no member can be compelled to participate in a military operation that it does not support. There is therefore no guarantee that the allies will respond to any given political or military challenge, particularly as alliance membership grows larger and more diverse. But NATO can be used to build political consensus and create military options to implement political goals. The allies would have fewer credible military options if their military leaders and forces were not working together on a day-to-day basis, developing interoperability of those forces, planning for contingency operations, and exercising their military capabilities. This daily routine develops political and military patterns of cooperation that underpin the ability to work together under pressure and, more importantly, under fire.

Defense Cooperation and Burden-sharing

NATO can also serve as a way to ensure that allies carry a fair share of the burdens of maintaining international peace. During the cold war, some Americans saw NATO as a creator of burdens for the United States rather than as an instrument for sharing them. Some still hold this view, particularly in light of the growing gap between U.S. and European military capabilities. On the one hand, the U.S. military presence in Europe, now under 100,000 troops on shore, is increasingly oriented toward force projection and peace operations rather than toward defense of European territory. The NATO framework provides the United States with leverage to push for additional European defense efforts, presuming the Europeans want the United States to remain involved in European security, which they apparently do. On the other hand, it could be argued that the habit of European security dependence on the United States is perpetuated by NATO, and that new means of cooperation, for example by giving the EU a homegrown role in defense, are needed to increase European self-reliance and reduce U.S. burdens.

Defense Cooperation and Political Change

NATO defense cooperation is now being used more prominently for political goals beyond its members' borders. Perhaps it is for this reason that some see NATO as becoming "more political." The Partnership for Peace (PFP) was initiated in 1994 to develop cooperation with non-NATO states. Through the partnership, Europe's new democracies have been learning how to develop systems of democratically controlled armed forces, as well as habits of cooperation with NATO nations and neighboring partners. The partnership approach helped the Czech Republic, Hungary and Poland meet the requirements for NATO membership and remains the principal path by which other nations can prepare to enter the alliance. Countries that were "neutrals" during the cold war are using the PFP to participate in NATO's efforts to promote stability in and around Europe. NATO's "Mediterranean Dialogue" seeks to reach out to non-NATO countries on the Mediterranean's southern rim to promote cooperation and stability in the region.

The allies are also using political/military cooperation with Russia as a means to change Russian perceptions of the alliance and, it is hoped, to change the political relationship between Moscow and NATO by gradually integrating Russia into a cooperative Euro-Atlantic security system. In a sense, the 1997 Founding Act with Russia (see Relations with Russia, p. 42) updated NATO's attempt to promote improved relations with Moscow, which had been prominently advanced in the 1967 Harmel Report. The strengthening of that tie today continues the process. If NATO succeeds, the defense cooperation relationship with Russia, which began with military cooperation in Bosnia, could leapfrog over the arms-control accords that were designed during the cold war to regulate relationships between parties that otherwise were in conflict with one another. Moving from a Russia-NATO relationship governed by arms control to one characterized by the transparent, predictable and confidence-building nature of defense cooperation would certainly mark a sea change in the European security system.

Acceptance of New Members

The drafters of the North Atlantic Treaty made it clear in Article 10 that accession to the treaty would remain open to "any other European state in a position to further the principles of this treaty and to contribute to the security of the North Atlantic area." This "open door" policy led to the membership of Greece and Turkey in 1951, West Germany in 1955, and Spain in 1982. After the countries of Central and Eastern Europe had freed themselves from communism and had begun establishing democratic systems of government, rejection of their desire for membership in NATO would have repudiated everything for which the North Atlantic Treaty has stood since 1949. Acceptance by the allies of the Czech Republic, Hungary and Poland in 1999, and of other qualified nations in the coming years, illustrates the fact that NATO is organized around transcendent values and goals that do not require an "enemy" to validate their continuing relevance.

A Stabilizing Influence

It is clear that NATO serves a variety of purposes for individual member states beyond these broadly stated goals. Many such "secondary" agendas help explain why current members want the alliance to continue, and why so many countries want to join. For example, former members of the 1955 Warsaw Pact (the military alliance led by the Soviet Union) do not fear attack from today's Russia, but they see NATO as a guarantee against falling once again into the Russian sphere of influence, as well as an insurance policy against any future resurgence of a Russian threat. Most European governments hope that the process of European unification will lead to more intensive security and defense cooperation among European states. But they continue to see the transatlantic link as essential to security in and around Europe.

Further, many Europeans believe that the U.S. role in Europe, particularly as translated by NATO, provides an important ingredient of stability that facilitates cooperation among European states. For example, even though Berlin is not seen as a threat by its neighbors, both Germany and nearby countries feel more comfortable with its role in Europe thoroughly integrated into the framework of both the EU and the transatlantic alliance. Skeptics today argue, however, that the United

States is no longer needed to help stabilize Europe, particularly as the EU assumes a growing role on the Continent.

Cooperative European Security

A question that frequently arises in the NATO debate is whether or not NATO is a collective-security organization. According to its classic definition, "collective security" is a system of interstate relations designed to maintain a balance of power and interests among the members that ensures peaceful relationships within that system. The League of Nations, established after World War I, is usually regarded as such a system.

NATO was from the outset designed as a system of cooperation among member states to deal with challenges and problems originating outside that system, not within it. Granted, NATO has to some extent tried to promote peaceful settlement of problems within the system. It helped heal World War

AP/Wide World Photos

Riga, Latvia, July 5, 2002: U.S. Senator Trent Lott (R-Miss.) addressed conference of NATO candidates—10 former East-bloc countries that he strongly endorsed for membership but warned of alliance concerns over their corruption and religious intolerance.

II wounds inflicted by Nazi Germany on its neighbors. NATO has served to mitigate conflicts between Greece and Turkey. The Russia-NATO Founding Act, the Partnership for Peace, and the Euro-Atlantic Partnership Council, established by NATO to promote security cooperation and consultation with all European states, have all helped maintain peaceful and co-operative relations among all states in Europe.

Such efforts enhance collective security and make it less likely that any NATO country will be attacked by any other European nation. When the allies began preparing for enlargement, they made clear to potential applicants that they must resolve differences with their neighbors in order to be seriously considered for NATO membership. The NATO countries insist that new members leave their old baggage of bilateral and ethnic differences with their neighbors by the wayside when they join NATO.

From a legal perspective, NATO does not have principal responsibility for collective security in Europe—the North Atlantic Treaty does not suggest such a role. In fact, the Organization for Security and Cooperation in Europe (formed in 1973 as the Conference on Security and Cooperation in Europe; known as OSCE since December 1994) was designed to promote peaceful relations among states "from the Atlantic to the Urals." The 1975 Helsinki Final Act established a series of agreed principles or "rules of the road " to govern relations among states in Europe. The OSCE member states (all European states and all the republics of the former Soviet Union, plus the United States and Canada) have adopted further agreements and principles, given the organization some diplomatic tools for conflict prevention, and convene regular meetings to try to nip problems in the bud.

3

Transatlantic Defense Ties

NATO's EVOLUTION over the past decade has responded to the changing international environment. The process of adaptation has already added new and complex missions to NATO's role, challenging alliance military leaders and forces to develop new capabilities as well as increased political sensitivity and awareness. NATO's accumulating experiences in the Balkans—first Bosnia-Herzegovina, Kosovo and then Macedonia—placed new and demanding requirements on the alliance. The struggle against terrorism now seems likely to bring even more dramatic changes.

These missions are more complex militarily and much more

Javier Solana, EU foreign and security policy chief meeting with NATO Secretary General Lord Robertson in Brussels, September 2000— the first meeting between NATO ambassadors and their European counterparts for defense and security.

diverse politically than the old cold-war collective-defense mission, even though the potential costs of failure during that period were a lot higher than they are today. NATO's military leaders and forces must accomplish these missions with significantly fewer resources than those available during the cold war. These missions require forces that are much more flexible and agile.

The question is whether political leaders in NATO countries will provide the resources to prepare forces for diverse operations and supply the political will required to make the most effective use of those forces.

During the 1990s, NATO's day-to-day activities became almost entirely dominated by new roles and missions. Nevertheless, many NATO members and military officials, as well as the U.S. Congress, continued to believe strongly that collective defense should remain NATO's "core mission." The logic for retaining collective defense as NATO's primary purpose goes beyond simply clinging to the old and familiar (although this tendency plays a part as well). There are some strong substantial reasons for keeping collective defense at the heart of the alliance.

First, something can be said for the role of the collective-defense commitment as an insurance policy against a new Russian threat emerging in the future. Under current circumstances, it cannot be excluded that, irrespective of the good will of NATO countries, future Russian leaders will choose some form of confrontational relationship with NATO rather than cooperation. Keeping NATO's collective-defense commitment alive reassures those allies that would be most exposed to a more aggressive Russia and also could serve as a deterrent to a Russian choice of confrontation over cooperation.

Secondly, new threats could once again bring the collective-defense commitment into play. Turmoil to the south and east of Europe, in North Africa and the Middle East, fed by various forms of extremism antagonistic toward the NATO countries and their values, combined with modern weapons of mass destruction and their delivery systems, could produce direct threats to the security of NATO countries. This point was brought home all too sharply with the September 11, 2001, terrorist attacks on the United States and the military campaign against the terrorist organizations in Afghanistan that followed. The NATO collective-defense commitment provides reassurance and potential deterrence, and also a rationale for allied cooperation in trying to mitigate or eliminate such threats through diplomacy and other means.

Third, and perhaps most important from a practical perspective, NATO's collective-defense commitment helps sustain a core of war-fighting military capabilities around which conflict-management capabilities can be built, and without which conflict-management policies would appear much less credible. It also provides a continuing rationale for the integrated command structure, without which critical day-to-day cooperation among allied militaries would dissipate, eventually undermining the ability of NATO countries to operate in coalition formations. Former head of the NATO Military Committee General Klaus Naumann argued during the late 1990s that the collective-defense mission and military capabilities of NATO were essential to its future. If all NATO countries developed forces capable of no more than peacekeeping operations, the alliance would become largely irrelevant to contingencies like those already seen in Bosnia and Kosovo.

Finally, NATO's collective-defense commitment carries with it a degree of serious intent and political will that would not be demonstrated by a less-demanding form of cooperation. Article 5, in effect, constitutes a statement by all the allies that they consider their security to be indivisible. It serves as a clear demonstration that the political values and goals articulated in the North Atlantic Treaty's preamble remain as valid for allied governments today as they were in 1949.

Will sufficient resources be made available by allied governments to implement a multiple-mission approach? Will the emerging gap in deployed military technologies between the United States and Europe increasingly impede coalition operations, creating a dual or three-tier alliance?

The EU's New Defense Role

One of the challenges for the United States and Europe is to ensure that the process of developing a more unified EU defense capability strengthens, not weakens, the alliance.

A central feature of the original transatlantic treaty had been the pledge of the European allies to work toward greater political, economic and defense cooperation among their separate nations. For many years, the search for greater European political unity was caught up in debates over the purposes and methods of cooperation. Finally, in 1970 the European Community (EC), the precursor of today's European Union, members agreed to initiate a process of European Political Cooperation (EPC). Over the years, the members of the EC expanded the scope and content of their consultations to the point where, by the end of the cold war, the EPC had become a regular and accepted part of the process of foreign-policy formulation in the member governments.

This expansion of topics and problems covered by the political consultations inevitably led the EC in the direction of "security policy." The EC members consciously stopped short of what could be considered "military policy." But EC consultations by the mid-1980s regularly included issues that were on NATO's consultative agenda as well.

U.S. policy toward European defense cooperation—largely a theoretical question in the 1980s—took a "yes, but" approach. Yes, the United States continued to support the process of European integration, but efforts to coordinate military/security cooperation should not undermine NATO.

In spite of U.S. concerns, NATO's December 1991 new strategic concept supported the goal of the European members assuming greater responsibility for their own security, while ensuring that NATO remained "...the essential forum for consultation among its members and the venue for agreement on policies bearing on the security and defense commitments of allies under the Washington treaty." In the wake of NATO's new strategic concept, the members of the EC signed in 1992 the Maastricht Treaty, transforming the EC into the European Union. The treaty included a commitment to "define and implement a common foreign and security policy."

In the autumn of 1998, British Prime Minister Tony Blair decided to make a major push for an EU role in defense. In several speeches, Blair bemoaned the fact that Europe's ability for autonomous military action was so limited and called for major institutional and resource innovations to make Europe a more equal partner in the transatlantic alliance.

In December 1998, Blair and French President Jacques Chirac met in St. Malo, France. The resulting St. Malo declaration envisioned creation of a Common European Security and Defense Policy, with the means and mechanisms to permit the EU nations to act "autonomously" should NATO decide not to act in some future scenario requiring military action.

The Clinton Administration's formal reaction took the traditional form of the "yes, but" approach. Secretary of State Madeleine Albright formally declared the Administration's support but cautioned the Europeans against "the three D's": duplication, decoupling and discrimination. Albright said the allies should not duplicate what was already being done effectively in NATO. More fundamentally, the new European initiative should not in any way "decouple" or "delink" the United States from Europe in the alliance, or the European defense efforts from those coordinated through NATO. Finally, Albright insisted there be no discrimination against NATO allies who were not members of the EU.

The April 1999 Washington Summit communiqué and the 1999 NATO strategic concept reflected transatlantic agreement that European defense capabilities needed a serious shot in the arm and that it had to be done in ways consistent with the U.S. warnings. The St. Malo accord was endorsed by all EU members at meetings in Cologne, Germany (June 1999) and Helsinki, Finland (December 1999).

In Helsinki, the EU members declared their determination "to develop an autonomous capacity to take decisions and, where NATO as a whole is not engaged, to launch and conduct EU-led military operations in response to international crises." They noted that the process "will avoid unnecessary duplication and does not imply the creation of a European army." The EU members continued to reiterate that collective defense remained a NATO responsibility and would not be challenged by the new EU arrangements. They agreed on several substantial steps, called the Helsinki Headline Goals:

♦ to establish by 2003 a corps-size intervention force of up to 60,000 persons from EU member-state armed forces capable of deploying within 60 days and being sustained for at least one year;

♦ to create new political and military bodies to allow the European Council (the EU's member-state decisionmaking body) to provide political guidance and strategic direction to joint military operations;

◆ to develop modalities for full consultation, cooperation and transparency between the EU and NATO, taking into account the "needs" of all EU member states (particularly the fact that four EU members—Austria, Ireland, Finland, Sweden—are not NATO members);

◆ to make "appropriate" arrangements to allow non-EU European NATO members and others to contribute to EU military-crisis management;

◆ to establish a nonmilitary-crisis-management mechanism to improve coordination of EU and member-state political, economic and other nonmilitary instruments in ways that might mitigate the need to resort to the use of force or make military actions more effective when they become necessary.

In 2001, when George W. Bush assumed the U.S. presidency, British Prime Minister Blair hurried to Washington to reassure the new Administration that CESDP would not hurt NATO. The Bush Administration's reaffirmation of U.S. support for the CESDP initiative was necessary because the incoming Administration was known to have concerns similar to those expressed earlier by the Clinton Administration.

Following President Bush's meeting with Prime Minister Blair, the new Administration appeared to settle into a relatively passive approach toward CESDP. However, following the September 11 terrorist attacks on the United States, the depth of Washington's skepticism about European defense efforts became apparent. The Administration shifted its focus to capabilities that the European allies would be willing and able to contribute to the near- term requirements of the war against terrorism. Discussion of the longer-term impact of CESDP seemed a much lower priority.

The conduct of the war on terrorism has therefore raised serious questions about European priorities reflected in CESDP and in the depressed levels of European defense spending. Some Bush Administration officials have questioned the wisdom of counting on future improvements in European defense capabilities. Some Europeans, meanwhile, have questioned whether there is any way to keep up with the pace of improvements in U.S. defense capabilities and have raised the possibility of a "division of labor" in which the United States would take care of most "war-fighting" scenarios while Europeans looked after less-demanding military situations. This growing debate only added to the importance of greater clarity concerning what European military forces would or would not be able to do in the future, whether in NATO, the EU, or ad hoc coalition formations. It also raised the important question of whether Europeans should place priorities on developing their ability to function in NATO coalitions with the United States or on operating autonomously with the support of NATO and the United States.

On the one hand, a division of labor has a certain logic: why shouldn't the United States and its allies concentrate on doing what they do best? On the other hand, confirming such tendencies in policy could lead the United States and its allies in the wrong directions, exacerbating the current "gaps" in the alliance and encouraging the tendency toward divergent U.S. and European views on international security challenges and preferred responses.

The indisputable view that the Europeans are not doing enough on defense has been inappropriately transformed into a belief that they are not doing anything to improve defense capabilities. Although Europe could use much more investment in defense, the major European military establishments are aiming to be able to conduct future operations on the kind of high-tech battlefield that currently is the exclusive U.S. domain. Scheduled improvements in intelligence capabilities, surveillance, target identification and acquisition systems, as well as in "smart" weaponry over the next 15 years, if carried out, should produce European forces that are more capable of conducting operations in a great variety of battlefield conditions in coalition with the United States or, if necessary, on their own.

A U.S. decision to dismiss the goal of working in coalition with America's closest allies would have the effect of a self-fulfilling prophecy, convincing European politicians that it is not worth the effort to devote resources to building modern military capabilities. If the United States wants to have allies with whom to share the military and political burdens of future military operations, it must make a conscious decision to promote that objective, not deter it.

U.S. policy will play an important part in helping Europeans to decide on their defense role. The United States will have to make it clear that it continues to value having militarily capable allies and back that up with concrete decisions such as implementing the technology-transfer reforms NATO's Secretary General Lord Robertson has been urging. Such a move could help tip the balance in favor of development of meaningful twenty-first-century combat capabilities on the part of major European militaries.

Divergence on Missile Defense

Early in 2001, the new Bush Administration's strong commitment to development of missile defenses appeared to pose one of the most fundamental challenges to NATO unity in the history of the alliance. Experts wrote about the dangers of "strategic disconnect" from a United States that would insulate itself from missile threats and be able to isolate itself from security problems around the world and to disengage from security in Europe. Missile-defense proponents, on the other hand, argued that if the United States could protect itself from rogue-state or terrorist-launched missile threats it would be in a better position to come to the aid of its allies in Europe and elsewhere.

The United States concluded that the September 11 events warranted the search for effective defenses against ballistic missiles as part of the overall threat posed by terrorists and rogue states. Public opinion, strongly supporting the war against terrorism and demonstrating the will to take casualties to achieve the war's objectives, also demonstrated increased support for developing missile defenses. For example, in the wake of the attacks, a poll by the Gallup organization found that some 70 percent of the adults questioned supported spending money to develop defenses against nuclear missiles. That was up from 53 percent in favor a year before.

However, not all aspects of the post-September 11 situation necessarily support more rapid development of missile defenses. The costs of the war in Afghanistan, other aspects of the war against terrorism and of enhanced homeland security will all compete with missile defense funding. In addition, the fact that Russia's President Vladimir Putin has been helpful in the war against terrorism has strengthened Putin's relationship with President Bush and increased the incentives for developing the U.S. missile defense program in ways that are compatible with continued U.S.-Russian cooperation on other issues. Moreover, test programs for missile defense technologies have still not demonstrated the level of success likely to be required to move systems toward full-fledged deployment.

4

Changing
Transatlantic Ties

THE PROCESS OF ADDING new members to the alliance following the end of the cold war was one that the allies approached carefully and with some trepidation. The new democracies that were just getting established in Eastern and Central Europe wanted as quickly as possible to be integrated into Western institutions to protect them against future attempts by Russia to assert its influence and control, as well as to help strengthen their fledgling democratic, free-market systems.

Many would have preferred that the EU take the lead in the enlargement process, bringing the new democracies into the

Western fold without provoking Russia, as their inclusion in NATO seemed likely to do. However, even though NATO membership brought with it requirements and obligations, they were not nearly as difficult or inflexible as those required by EU membership. NATO is not an integrative body—its members all participate as sovereign states, without any commitment to sacrifice any of that sovereignty, at least in a legal fashion. The EU, on the other hand, has already integrated most aspects of economic interaction among the members who have given up sovereignty over many aspects of economic, financial and trade policy. In addition, the gaps between the economies of Eastern and Central Europe and those of Western Europe were huge. The new democracies were paying the double price incurred by the process of creating an economy driven by market forces on top of the residual costs of the failed centrally directed economic institutions and practices that were being replaced.

And so, NATO took the lead on enlargement, inviting the Czech Republic, Hungary and Poland to join the alliance, which they did in 1999. At that point, the enlargement process was paused to allow time for Russia to adapt to the emerging new reality of Western incursion into what had not so long ago been a zone of Soviet control, as well as to give NATO time to carefully examine the impact of enlargement on the alliance itself.

In the next several years, additional countries will likely begin the process of joining the alliance. They include Slovenia and Slovakia, Bulgaria and Romania, and the Baltic states—former republics of the Soviet Union—Estonia, Latvia and Lithuania. Most of these countries do not meet all the guidelines laid out in NATO's 1996 study on enlargement, which was supposed to guide the process. Some have not completed the process of making their military establishments compatible with civilian control in a democratic political system; most are not prepared to make major military contributions to the alliance; for a few, there are questions about

Kirk@The Blade

the depth of their support for democracy and free-market economic systems.

At the same time, the process of EU enlargement is moving ahead slowly but surely. Over one dozen countries—Bulgaria, Cyprus, the Czech Republic, Estonia, Hungary, Latvia, Lithuania, Malta, Poland, Romania, the Slovak Republic, Slovenia and Turkey—are engaged in the process. Several will join the EU in the next few years.

The next stage of NATO enlargement raises several questions. Will further enlargement handcuff NATO's consensus-based decisionmaking process and turn it into a mainly "political" organization, incapable of concerted military action? Does the Bush Administration's support for such a substantial enlargement suggest that it does not care whether or not NATO loses its capacity for coordinating military actions? If this next enlargement disturbs relations with Russia while simultaneously weakening NATO, will it receive the advice and consent of the U.S. Senate during the required ratification process?

Relations with Russia

The military and ideological threat posed by the Soviet Union, along with European concerns about a resurgent Germany, provided the original stimulus for the transatlantic alliance. When the Soviet Union imploded at the end of the cold war, the United States and its European allies decided that even though this founding threat was disappearing, the cooperation that had developed over the years was not only based on solid common values and interests, but also had continuing utility in a post-Soviet world.

Russia continued to be a major factor in allied calculations. In spite of its devastated economy and military forces so weakened as to be incapable of putting down rebellion in the former Soviet Republic of Chechnya, Russia remained a world-class nuclear power and a huge variable in Europe's future. The development of a liberal democratic system in Russia would constitute a dramatic gain for international peace and stability. An autocratic, deprived and dissatisfied Russia would constitute a major source of instability for the indefinite future. As a consequence, the allies moved carefully throughout the 1990s, trying to assess how steps that they were taking to adapt their alliance would affect and be affected by Russia.

As the EU and NATO began their separate processes of outreach to the new democracies emerging in Eastern and Central Europe, neither thought Russia would soon qualify for membership in either organization. It was clear, however, that Russia, weak as it was, remained an important player in European security.

NATO reached out to Russia as it moved toward including the Soviet Union's former Central and East European "allies" in the Western security system. Russia was offered participation in NATO's partnership program and then, in the context of the first round of NATO enlargement, was given a special relationship to the alliance with negotiation of "The Founding Act on Mutual Relations, Cooperation and Security between NATO and the Russian Federation," establishing a Permanent

Joint Council (PJC)—NATO nations plus Russia—as a framework for continuing consultations.

Russia's acceptance of the PJC was grudging. Russian leaders wanted something more—something that would acknowledge Moscow's importance in European security. The NATO countries, on the other hand, did not want to give Russia a direct say in deliberations and certainly not a veto over their actions—a concern directly expressed by American conservatives during the 1990s debate on NATO enlargement.

However, under the leadership of President Putin, a democratically elected but autocratic leader with pragmatic foreign-policy inclinations, Russia and NATO have moved toward a more meaningful relationship. The most important stimulus was provided by the September 11 terrorist attacks and Putin's offer of assistance in the U.S.-declared war against terrorism. Putin's position clearly facilitated work toward U.S.-Russia agreements on dramatic cuts in strategic-nuclear-weapons arsenals and possible agreements on missile defenses. Putin also hinted at new perspectives on Russia's relationship to NATO and its attitude toward NATO enlargement.

British Prime Minister Blair, who had played such an important role in getting the EU's CESDP on track, started the ball rolling for a fresh Russia-NATO initiative by proposing a new forum for Russia-NATO cooperation. Blair, in a letter to NATO Secretary General Lord Robertson, suggested creation of a "Russia/North Atlantic Council," which would make decisions by consensus on certain issues affecting both NATO and Russia, such as terrorism, arms proliferation and peacekeeping.

Apparently with the blessing of the Bush Administration, Secretary General Robertson put the idea forward during an official visit to Moscow.

The initiative was met by headlines blaring that "Russia Could Get Veto Power in New NATO." Russian conservatives worried that Putin was about to give away the store, while other Russian analysts speculated that the move would give Russia associate membership in the alliance. American conservatives were concerned that the move might do in NATO. Polish observers fretted that this might be the first step toward Russian membership in NATO. French observers wondered if events were moving too fast for rational consideration of their consequences.

In spite of such arguments, on May 28, 2002, at a NATO-Russia summit meeting outside Rome, Italy, the allies agreed to establish a new council to identify and pursue opportunities for joint action between Russia and the NATO allies. The leaders made it clear that the new council would not give Russia a veto over NATO decisions.

The Permanent Joint Council was replaced by a new NATO-Russia Council, which will meet more regularly and will focus particularly on counterterrorism, nonproliferation and containing regional hostilities. However, the regular agenda of the North Atlantic Council will not be shifted to the new framework. The NAC will decide when issues should be submitted to decision by the NATO-Russia Council. If the NATO-Russia Council becomes deadlocked on an issue because of Russian disagreement, this will not block the NATO members from acting in the NAC without Russian agreement or participation. Russia will not have a "veto" over NATO decisions, even though it clearly will exercise more influence on those decisions than previously.

The way in which the new arrangement will work depends largely on political judgments made in Moscow and in NATO-member governments. Lord Robertson argues that the real differences between the former "19 + 1" arrangement and a new "20" forum is a matter of "chemistry rather than arithmetic, as even the best format and seating arrangements can be no substitute for genuine political will and an open mind on both sides."

The advent of a more meaningful, action-oriented NATO-Russia relationship could be a very positive development for European security. It will not block NATO decisions on enlargement of the alliance. In fact, just as creation of the PJC

Russian President Vladimir Putin and NATO Secretary General
Lord Robertson are flanked by Italian Premier Silvio Berlusconi
and President George W. Bush at the site of the NATO-Russia
Council founding.

with Russia "accompanied" and facilitated the first round of
NATO enlargement, development of the new NATO-Russia
Council will parallel implementation of NATO's next enlarge-
ment round. The step will not presage imminent Russian mem-

bership in the alliance. Militarily, Russia obviously could make major contributions to the alliance. However, Russia's size and importance suggest that geopolitical factors will play a large role in deciding when Russia might be acceptable as a member. Politically, Russia is a long way from meeting the guidelines for membership laid out in NATO's 1995 Study on Enlargement. Russia falls far short, particularly in terms of the internal development of liberal democratic institutions, including a free press and a Western-style human-rights regime. If Russia some day meets these guidelines, there truly will be a "new world order" and Russia may then be considered a legitimate candidate for membership. Until then, there will likely remain a clear distinction between what issues are decided with members of the alliance and which are decided with this very important Russian partner.

The UN and the OSCE in Transatlantic Relations

The year 2002 saw the start of questioning NATO's relevance and the EU's potential for enhancing European military capabilities. Little has been said, however, about the continued relevance of the United Nations and the Organization for Security and Cooperation in Europe (OSCE), two other organizations important for transatlantic relations. Both these institutions fall into the gap between current U.S. and European attitudes toward multilateral cooperation and institutions.

The UN has in recent years been out of favor with American conservatives. The UN therefore has a fairly low priority with the Bush Administration. In Europe, however, the UN is still seen as the most important forum for validation of the use of force internationally. In the late 1990s, the United States and its allies debated whether or not NATO could, or should, act without a mandate from the UN Security Council. The Europeans insisted that a UN mandate should be the rule, but accepted U.S. arguments that the war against Serbian forces in Kosovo would be conducted without such a mandate, given Russian and Chinese opposition to the campaign. The Bush

Administration is even more adamant than the Clinton Administration about the need to be flexible and not to insist on a UN mandate. The September 11 terrorist attacks may have moved the Europeans slightly toward the U.S. position, but their preference remains in favor of using force internationally only with a UN mandate. This issue raised its head once again with regard to a possible attack on Iraq, creating tensions between a unilaterally predisposed United States and a multilaterally leaning Europe.

The OSCE makes few headlines and does not play a major role in U.S. foreign policy considerations, but it is an important part of the European security landscape. Starting out as the Conference on Security and Cooperation in Europe during the cold war, with all European states, Canada and the United States participating, the CSCE provided a broad framework to guide relations among states and between states and their citizens. At the end of the cold war, it was transformed from a meeting process into an organization which has helped establish post-conflict stability in the Balkans, monitors elections in new democracies, promotes transparency in military affairs, and generally provides the "rules of the road" for relations among states in Europe. The OSCE's role may diminish as functioning democracies are established throughout Europe and the majority of states join NATO and the EU. However, it seems likely that the OSCE will have a role to play in facilitating the establishment of peace, human rights and democracy in the Balkans and to Europe's southeast in the Caucasus region for many years to come. This process inevitably will be of greater interest to the European allies than to the United States, but seems unlikely to be a source of serious transatlantic differences.

The Middle East as a Source of Friction

One of the most difficult issues between the United States and Europe is how to deal with the bloody conflict in the Middle East. Historically, the United States has carried the main burden of support for the peace process there and has exercised the preponderant external influence on the key players: Israel, the Palestinians and the Arab states in the region. Europe has aspired to a greater role and economically has become a major player in the region. But the Europeans have not been able to muster the political and military clout necessary to play a decisive role in the Middle East peace process.

The initial decision by the Bush Administration to back away from the active role that the Clinton Administration had played on behalf of a Middle East peace settlement might have seemed warranted to the new Administration as it looked at the frustrating record of previous U.S. efforts to broker peace in the region. However, the belief that the peace process could continue on its own dynamic was mistaken, and the region descended into a conflict of suicide/homicide bomb attacks by young Palestinians on civilian Israeli targets and brutal retaliation by the Israeli government. By the time the Administration had decided to reengage the United States in efforts to arrange a cease-fire to help get the peace process back on track, the conflict had moved many steps further away from the peace that had been sought in earlier U.S. attempts by the Clinton Administration and its predecessors.

The fundamental transatlantic problem is created by the fact that the United States serves as the ultimate guarantor for the survival of Israel, surrounded as it is by governments and peoples largely hostile to its existence, while the policy of the European allies is generally less sympathetic to Israel and claims to be more "evenhanded" with regard to the Israeli-Palestinian dispute. The extent to which the United States "automatically" supports Israel can be exaggerated, but it is true that the large and influential U.S. Jewish community exercises considerable influence in Washington. That, combined with the U.S. moral commitment to Israel's survival, does play a role in shaping U.S. Mideast policy. And, even though Palestinian and Arab leaders believe that U.S. policy is biased against the Palestinians, they understand that only the United States can exercise sufficient clout with Israel to promote the eventual formation of a Palestinian state. This point was brought home clearly in the spring of 2002 when Israel denied a high-level EU delegation access to Palestine Liberation Organization leader Yasir Arafat, whom Israeli forces had physically isolated in his headquarters in Jerusalem.

The bottom line is that the United States and its European allies are working toward the same goals: peace, secure borders for Israel and a state for the Palestinians. The problem is that there is no guaranteed or easy route to that outcome. Failures along the way produce disagreement as to ways and means, and the different U.S. and European perspectives and responsibilities in the Middle East create friction in the alliance. Until there is a peaceful solution, the United States and Europe inevitably will disagree about how to get there, but any final settlement will likely require the diplomatic, military and economic resources of the United States and Europe as a foundation for a lasting solution.

The Iraq Challenge

During 2002, what to do about the dictatorial Iraqi regime led by Saddam Hussein became the most difficult issue on the transatlantic agenda. The Bush Administration concluded that Saddam should be removed from power to ensure that his regime could no longer develop weapons of mass destruction (chemical, biological and nuclear) or support terrorist operations. The United States appeared headed toward an invasion of Iraq with or without approval from the UN Security Council or support from U.S. allies. British Prime Minister Blair shared the Bush Administration's concern about the threat posed by Saddam and the need to take decisive action. But most European leaders preferred first getting UN weapons inspectors back in Iraq to try one last time to disarm the Iraqi leader through peaceful means. They saw the largely unilateral U.S. approach as dangerously undermining the entire system of international law and cooperation that previous U.S. Presidents had helped construct. German Chancellor Gerhard Schroeder, in a close reelection race (which he won), went to the extreme of saying that Germany would not support an attack on Iraq either militarily or financially.

In spite of the large gap between the U.S. and European policy preferences, American and European public opinion were closely aligned, judging that the United States should attack Iraq only with a UN mandate and the support of U.S. allies. However, the policy debate intensified existing feelings that the United States and Europe were moving in different directions internationally, calling into question the alliance that had been so important to their interests for over 50 years.

The Outlook for Transatlantic Relations

Broadly conceived, there are three possible scenarios for the future of transatlantic relations. Because the United States and Europe are so closely tied, there seems little chance that they will allow the current or future crises to deteriorate into a "divorce." If this is so, then the worst-case outcome is for the partners to drift toward a grudging "marriage of convenience." A middle road would be a course of continuity and adaptation, keeping the relationship on a steady course without dramatic changes. The third possibility might be to grow the current relationship into a much closer cooperation community.

A "marriage of convenience" could be the consequence of allowing serious problems in the relationship to fester without seeking accommodations and compromise approaches. U.S.-European differences on issues such as the death penalty, spending on welfare programs, hormone additives to food products and other social, moral and life-style preferences would reveal U.S. and European values as divergent. The United States would give low priority to development assistance and Third World aid, while the Europeans made foreign assistance a leading element in their foreign policy. The United States would rely increasingly on the use of its military power to resolve international problems or simply to get its way internationally, while the Europeans focused mainly on providing forces to help keep the peace. NATO would become increasingly irrelevant as the Europeans mounted their peacekeeping operations through the EU and the United States conducted mainly unilateral military operations or acted as the leader of ad hoc coalitions.

A course of continuity and adaptation would find the United States and Europe dedicated to preserving a good working relationship. This would be based on the analysis that the alliance remains important to both and that the "crisis" is simply another bump in the road. In this case, careful attention and evolutionary adaptation will keep the relationship vital and effective. The financial and economic ties remain self-correcting, as mutual interests will dictate that differences be resolved in a way that, on balance over time, benefits both. The "social" and "moral" gaps between U.S. and European thinking will be largely issues on which there are also divisions inside the United States as well as among Europeans. They present some difficult choices, but do not represent fundamental and clear splits between the United States and Europe. In this scenario, NATO will remain relevant if the European allies take the necessary steps to improve their defense efforts and the United States pays more attention to the requirements for successful coalition military operations.

A more radical eventuality would be based on the assessment that transatlantic relations remain critically important to both the United States and Europe but that they are in a crisis that requires dramatic action. Successful continuation depends on more far-reaching moves to strengthen transatlantic bonds. NATO's integrated command structure could be reorganized to focus more clearly on the alliance's new functions in the war against terrorism and other global military challenges. Perhaps more importantly, the allies could appoint a committee of "wise men" to prepare a new Atlantic Community Treaty to include political, economic and other areas of cooperation not falling within NATO's formal mandate.

The transatlantic relationship cannot be taken for granted on either side of the Atlantic—it is simply too important for both the United States and Europe.

Talking It Over

A Note for Students and Discussion Groups

This issue of the HEADLINE SERIES, like its predecessors, is published for every serious reader, specialized or not, who takes an interest in the subject. Many of our readers will be in classrooms, seminars or community discussion groups. Particularly with them in mind, we present below some discussion questions—suggested as a starting point only—and references for further reading, as well as pertinent online resources.

Discussion Questions

Are the values articulated in the North Atlantic Treaty still valid for both the United States and Europe? Do current differences over trade issues, U.S. unilateral tendencies and the sanctity of international law threaten to undermine the sense of shared values?

Does the United States need allies when it can conduct most military operations with its own forces? Does it matter to the American people whether or not other democratic countries support U.S. approaches to the resolution of international issues? What are the costs and benefits of going it alone internationally or, alternatively, of taking multilateral approaches to foreign problems?

How will U.S.-European differences over policy toward Iraq affect broader transatlantic relations?

How important are the European allies to the United States? Are they still the most valuable U.S. allies or are other countries now more useful, and in what ways?

Does Europe need to act independently and "autonomously" in order to validate the process of European integration? Is it contradictory for Europe to pursue greater political and military integration while at the same time strengthening transatlantic cooperation with the United States and Canada?

What is NATO's role in the twenty-first-century world? Is NATO becoming largely a "political" organization used to help spread democracy and stability across Europe, or does it still play important military roles?

Russia's President Putin has brought his country into a much closer relationship with NATO. What are Putin's motivations for this step? What does he expect Russia will get in return? Will it tend to make NATO less or more effective politically and militarily?

As NATO admits new members, will it become less and less capable of making decisions, given the fact that it operates on the basis of consensus? Does U.S. support for a substantial enlargement of NATO's membership indicate that the Bush Administration no longer cares whether or not NATO is an effective military organization?

Do the United States and Europe need to take radical steps, for example, by forming a broader Atlantic Community to enhance political and economic cooperation, in order to ensure the future well-being of transatlantic relations?

Annotated Reading List

Brenner, Michael, and Parmentier, Guillaume, *Reconcilable Differences: U.S.-French Relations in the New Era*. Washington, DC, Brookings Institution Press, 2002. Examines the difficult but important U.S.-French security relationship.

Goldgeier, James M., *Not Whether But When, The U.S. Decision to Enlarge NATO*. Washington, DC, Brookings Institution Press, 1999. Study of U.S. decisionmaking on the admission of the Czech Republic, Hungary and Poland to NATO.

Gordon, Philip H., and Steinberg, James B., *NATO Enlargement: Moving Forward; Expanding the Alliance and Completing Europe's Integration*. Washington, DC, Brookings Institution Press, November 2001. Looks ahead to the next stages of NATO enlargement.

Howorth, Jolyon, *European Integration and Defence: The Ultimate Challenge?* Paris, France, EU Institute for Security Studies, Chaillot Paper No. 43, November 2000. Analyzes the process of creating a European Union defense capability.

Hunter, Robert Edwards, *The European Security and Defense Policy: NATO's Companion—or Competitor?* Santa Monica, CA, RAND Corporation, 2002. Well-informed U.S. perspective on EU-NATO defense relations.

Kagan, Robert, "Power and Weakness," *Policy Review*, June-July 2002. Explores the different U.S. and European approaches to the use of force.

Kaplan, Lawrence S., *The Long Entanglement: NATO's First Fifty*

Years. Westport, CT, Praeger Publishers, 1999. Classic scholarly analysis of NATO's history.

Kay, Sean, *NATO and the Future of European Security*. Lanham, MD., Rowman & Littlefield Publishers, Inc., 1998. A political analysis of the dynamics of transatlantic relations.

Lindley-French, Julian, *Terms of Engagement: the Paradox of American Power and the Transatlantic Dilemma post-11 September*. Paris, France, EU Institute for Security Studies, Chaillot Paper No. 52, May 2002.

Rühle, Michael, "Imagining NATO 2011," *NATO Review*, Autumn 2001. Lays out different possibilities for the future of European security arrangements.

Sloan, Stanley R., *NATO, the European Union and the Atlantic Community: The Transatlantic Bargain Reconsidered*. Lanham, MD., Rowman & Littlefield Publishers, Inc., 2002. An interpretive history of transatlantic relations and a perspective on the future of the Atlantic Community.

Yost, David S., *NATO Transformed: The Alliance's New Roles in International Security*. Washington, DC, United States Institute of Peace Press, 1998. Detailed analysis of changes in NATO in the 1990s.

Online Resources

Two key reference works for the study of the Atlantic Community are the NATO Handbook, *2001*, NATO Office of Information and Press, 1110 Brussels, Belgium, and *The History of the European Union: A Chronology from 1946 to 2002*, European Union, Brussels, Belgium. Updated NATO information is at **http://www.nato.int**; EU information is on the Europa website at **http://europa.eu.int**.

Other websites of interest include that of the EU Institute for Security Studies at **http://www.iss-eu.org**, where the Chaillot Papers are located; the Atlantic Council of the United States at **http://www.acus.org**; and the Atlantic Community Initiative at **http://www.atlanticcommunity.org**, where a "living history" of the Atlantic Community and related information can be found.

HEADLINE SERIES OF CURRENT INTEREST

■ **MEXICO: CHANGING OF THE GUARD**
by George W. Grayson
HS323, $5.95, 80 pp., Fall 2001. ISBN no: 0-87124-199-4.
Product ID no: 31510.

■ **PAKISTAN: FLAWED NOT FAILED STATE**
by Dennis Kux
HS322, $5.95, 88 pp., Summer 2001. ISBN no: 0-87124-198-6.
Product ID no: 31509.

■ **CLINTON AND CONGRESS: THE POLITICS OF FOREIGN POLICY**
by Terry L. Deibel
HS321, $5.95, 80 pp., Fall 2000. ISBN no: 0-87124-196-X.
Product ID no: 31506.

■ **INDIA: OLD CIVILIZATION IN A NEW WORLD**
by Barbara Crossette
HS320, $5.95, 88 pp., Spring 2000. ISBN no: 0-87124-193-5.
Product ID no: 31494.

FPA.org

GREAT DECISIONS ONLINE

Download the latest GD Updates, join a discussion group, access resources for using Great Decisions, find out about Great Decisions Television in your area or read the latest National Opinion Ballot Report.

GLOBAL FORUMS

Guides bring you nonpartisan analysis, links, the most up-to-the-minute information and online discussion on current global concerns.

FPA BOOKSTORE

You can order our HEADLINE SERIES, *Great Decisions,* Special Publications and the best of global affairs publishing in Editor's Picks in our secure, online bookstore.

JOB BOARD

Jobs and internships in global affairs organizations, including international nonprofits and government agencies.

GLOBAL VIEWS

Interviews, research, analysis, news, maps and organizations searchable by issue and region.

E-NEWSLETTERS

The latest in foreign policy sent to your In Box. Sign up for one of our free weekly newsletters today.

EVENTS

Global affairs events sponsored by FPA, the World Affairs Councils of America, international organizations and universities.

Connect to a community of global thinkers
Visit FPA.org today

DEC 1 2 2002

FOREIGN POLICY ASSOCIATION

470 Park Avenue South, 2nd Floor ■ New York, NY 10016-6819
Order Toll-Free (800) 477-5836 ■ Fax (212) 481-9275 ■ www.fpa.org

Sold to: (please print)

Name _____

School /Address _____

City _____ State _____ Zip _____

Daytime Phone _____

Ship to: (please print)

Name _____

School /Address _____

City _____ State _____ Zip _____

Daytime Phone _____

→ Prepayment must accompany all orders from individuals, and must include shipping and handling charges. Libraries, universities and schools using purchase orders may be billed. Orders placed for new accounts are subject to credit approval.

→ New York State residents please add 8.25% sales tax; Canadian residents please add 7% GST.

→ All orders outside the U.S. and its possessions must be prepaid in U.S. funds with a check drawn on a U.S. correspondent bank. Please include shipping and handling charges as noted below.

PUBLICATION	QTY.	UNIT PRICE	TOTAL

SHIPPING AND HANDLING	**SUBTOTAL**
Headline Series	
$2.50 first copy; $.50 each additional copy.	NYS and Canadian residents add sales tax
Great Decisions	
Domestic: Included in price of book	← Shipping and handling
Foreign (including Canada):	
$4.00 first copy; $1.00 each additional copy.	**TOTAL** $

METHOD OF PAYMENT:

❑ Check enclosed (payable to Foreign Policy Association)

❑ PO attached   ❑ American Express   ❑ Visa   ❑ Mastercard

Credit Card # _____

Expiration Date _____ Signature _____